BIRDWATCHER'S

MINDFULNESS MEDITATION
ADULT
COLORING BOOK

ASSEMBLED BY
MADDIE MAYFAIR

© December 2016

All rights reserved.

ISBN-13: 978-1540800565

ISBN-10: 1540800563

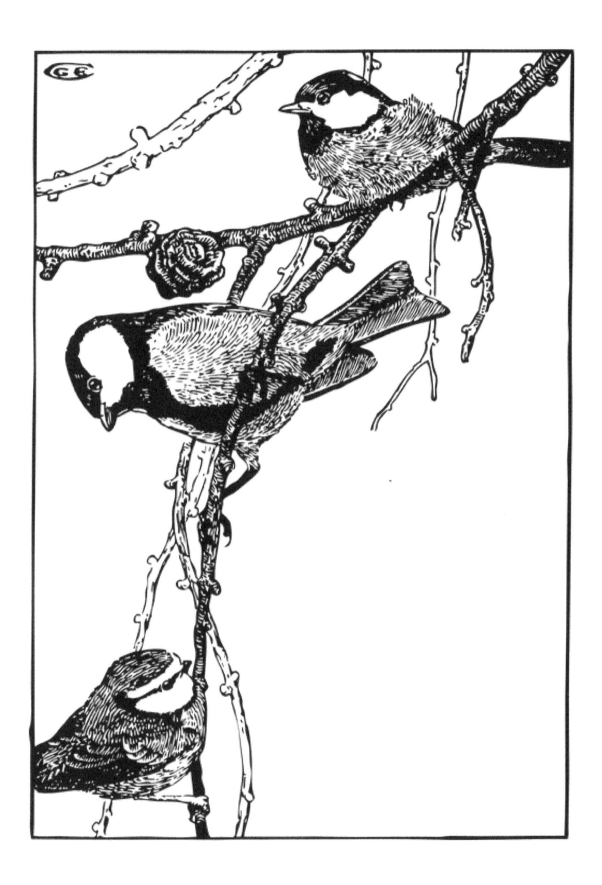

Enjoy even more *Colouring Books for Grown-Ups,* including:

Made in the USA
Coppell, TX
19 November 2020